I'VE LANDED
EMPRESS P

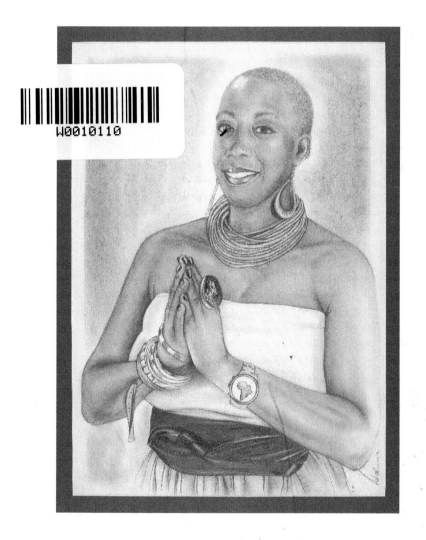

APS BOOKS
STOURBRIDGE

APS Books,
4 Oakleigh Road,
Stourbridge,
West Midlands,
DY8 2JX

APS Books is a subsidiary of
the APS Publications imprint

www.andrewsparke.com

ISBN 9781789960365

Cover artwork by Asher

Instagram @empressppoet
Twitter @empresspfg
Facebook Poetempressp

The verses contained in this book are also to be released in CD format also titled 'I've Landed'.

Praises to Jah The Almighty for my life.

Love to my son Andre and my rock Tony Roots, for being on this journey with me.

To all of you that have inspired and supported me on my path - More Culture, Sue Brown, Miss Culture Jam and many others.

Jah Blessings and Love.

CONTENTS

Why Do You Call Me A Baldhead?

Yes, my head hasn't long flowing locks, but see my stunning sculptured head, just like an African warrior.

Don't look at my baldhead, look at my shapely cheekbones, that when I smile you see my adorable dimples.

Don't look at my baldhead, look at my small, cute, flat Nubian nose, that remind you of my ancestry.

Don't look at my bald head, can't you see my luscious thick lips, that are soft to touch or kiss.

Don't look at my baldhead, look at my supple, smooth breasts, just right for suckling my offspring.

Don't look at my baldhead, what about my muscular gorgeous shaped shoulders, a pillow for friends and my man to cry or lean on.

Don't look at my baldhead, it's a distraction, look at my soft round belly, that carries my brood, that will continue my kin and tribe.

Don't look at my smooth baldhead, look at my curvaceous buttocks, that show you that I'm a black gal!!

Don't look at my baldhead, look at my strapping, defined legs, that walk back and forth from my fields with my harvest.

Don't look at my baldhead, can't you see my attractive gracious feet, smooth to touch, hold or kiss!

I may not have any hair to flick in your face, but look at this Majestic Nubian Empress.
You know what! Look pan my Baldhead!!!

What A Noise!

Birds twittering, twittering
Noisy,
Arguing,
Loud,
Having a conversation,
Chit chat, chit chat
Touching base with each other.
Are you having a union meeting?
Gosh so loud!
Twittering, twittering

Making such a din
in the morning,
before the sun rises
whoa!
Calling all your brothers and sisters
from near and far
Twittering, twittering

You're an alarm clock
All of you,
At the same time!
Can't you do it one at a time!
Twittering Twittering

Are you telling everyone to get up!!
Sun's Up!
Rise and Shine!
Don't waste the day,
There's a worm to catch,
Food for our bellies,
Twittering, Twittering

Remember Bob Marley 'Three Little Birds'
I heard fifty little birds this morning!
Twittering, twittering
Telling me
'Not to worry about a thing'!

Breeze

Gentle breeze swirling around my shoulders
Tender, saying hello to my face
Nature's way of cooling me down
With its soft kisses
On my ears
On my lips
On my cheeks
Letting me know,
I'm relaxing you
Making you still
Helping me
To forget my woes
Soothing me
Breeze I want to float in you
Drifting among your breath,
You're so warm,
Rocking me
Whispering to me
Relax,
Be Calm
Forget your sadness,
Breeze
Nature's way of
Making me still

Close Your Eyes

Close your eyes, hear the water rushing and bubbling
Close your eyes listen to the children laughing and giggling
Close your eyes catch the band in the background playing 'Summertime'
Close your eyes, you can hear conversations
'Do we have to go to work tomorrow?'
'Don't want to go to school'

Close my eyes, feel the waft of air on my face
Close your eyes, listen to the water gushing so vibrant
Close your eyes, can smell tanginess of barbecue food
Close my eyes, hearing the sound of high heels clicking on the concrete
Close your eyes, you can hear different dialects, is it German, French or
Patois
Close my eyes, can't hear the sun shining, but can feel its warmth
Close my eyes, where am I?
Montego Bay, Jamaica
Labada Beach, Ghana
Playa don Bossa, Ibiza
Open my eyes,
Brindley Place, Birmingham

Bass Trance

I need Bass
It's taking me over
Bass is powerful
Bass is intoxicating
Bass is a drug
Bass is putting me into a trance
Bass is making me move in unusual ways
Bass is in my bones and my veins

I'm in a Bass Trance

My arms are swinging to the Bass
My head is nodding to the Bass
My shoulders are swaying to the Bass
My hips are swinging to the Bass
My eyes are dazed by the Bass
I'm hypnotised by the Bass
I'm intoxicated by the Bass

I'm in a Bass Trance

I'm stamping my feet to the Bass
My toes are tingling to the Bass
My heart is vibrating to the Bass
My belly is rumbling to the Bass
My soul is loving the Bass
I'm in a Bass Trance

I'm in a Bass Trance
I'm in a Bass Trance

New Life

Staying alive
Hope
Land, road and sea
Taking a risk
Get food
Better chance
Swimming
War
Escaping to have a better life
Poverty
Want a safer life
Refugees
Economic
Migrants
Lampusaia
Malta
Crete
European Union
Dead bodies
Floating corpses
Unsafe boats
Overcrowded
Greedy traffickers
Motherless children
Mothers losing their children
Families lost
Lost
Desperation
Better future
Cold
Travelling across deserts
Crammed
No life jackets
Phones lost
Horizon can't be seen
No land in sight
No hope
Child corpses
Tragedy
All they wanted was a better life

Foot On Bus Seats

I'm vex
Put on my nice white pants with my classy silver sandals
Looking cris!
Looking forward to linking up with my crew

Get on the bus, don't go upstairs, sitting at the back downstairs
Looking stylish in my pristine white pants and silver sandals

Enjoying the bus ride,
Big smile on my face
I stand up to come off the bus,
In my cool white pants and bright silver sandals
A lady behind me says' look pan your pants'
I look down to see where the lady was pointing
I see a big brown mud mark, that was not there when I left my yard
I'm vex

Mud pan my sharp white pants, with my sliver sandals

I'm angry
What I'm saying right now
Take your dirty boots, trainers, flip-flops off the bloody seats on the bus,
train or tram.
The seats are for sitting on not for your 'dutty' footwear
I'm Vex!

Just Tell Me The Truth

Why when I ask you a question
I don't get a straight answer?
You're scared of my reaction
You think I'll shout at you
If I ask you if you are you fine?
You say Yes ,
but you mean No
Your face tell me so,
Your lips are pushed up
You confuse me
You tell me I should know what you're thinking
I'm not a mind reader
If I was
I would be a millionaire

Tell me if you are tired
Tell me if your day was hard
Tell me if you are in pain
All I want is honesty from you
Not mixed messages
This is confusing
In ten years time, you'll throw it back at me,
That I didn't listen to you,
But, you wasn't honest
When I ask you questions

Are you using your psyches on me?
You want to be in control of me?
I wonder if you want to mad me
Drive me crazy
Do you believe me when I say I love you?
You think I'm telling you lies?
You're trying to confuse me?
All I want is honesty
When I ask you a question
Just give me a straight answer.
If I'm pissing you off tell me?
If you don't like my company
just tell me to go?
All I want is for you to be straight with me.
You say you don't want to hurt my feelings,

I don't care
I want your honesty
Not lies
Remember
Honesty is the best policy

Fellow Habitants Trees

You grow with patience,
Do you talk to each other?
Do you know when to stop growing?
Your leaves look so beautiful, so lush
You start so small
Growing into marvellous structures
I bet you don't moan, you accept your growth so naturally
Not like us humans always complaining.
You've seen the changes over the years, even centuries
I bet you laugh at us, us humans
Get annoyed when we kill your brothers and sisters
Why do we do that?
You've been here longer than us,
I bet you can tell us a thing or two about survival, love and peace.
You look so sturdy
Powerful
Enduring all manner of storms
Your roots how far do you go?
Are you touching the earth's core?
In years you've continue to grow,
Surviving so much
Our polluted air that stifle your growth
Our rain that may be acid, that burn your leaves and bark
But still you grow
You are tough
Wherever a seed fall you grow
I'm humbled by your presence
When the breeze goes through your leaves, are you talking to the creator?
Or to your fellow tree?
I bet you laugh at us,
You've seen us come and go
But you've stood firm
Some of you are no longer with us,
Through our destruction of your forests, for our material gain
For what, our shelter, our buildings, our bridges, our paper, our food
How can we humans say thank you to you
Oh magnificent Tree

Universal Energy

Universal energy
Lift me
Raise me up
Cover me with your spirit
Enhance my soul

Universal energy
You are peace
You calm me
You love me

Universal energy,
My life force
My life source
My breath
My blood
My vibes

Universal energy
My connection to nature,
Other living and
breathing beings
I am part of you,

Universal Energy
You are
The sun,
The wind,
The sea,
The space
The air,
The earth

I am at peace with you
I give praises to you
Universal energy

Grass

Walking along,
Newtown Row
Grass just cut,

What a beautiful smell
Tingling in my nostrils,
Lush and fresh,
Grass just cut

Seeing the greenery,
In the Inner City
So lovely
Grass just cut

Tantalising
Refreshing
Scent of
Grass just cut

So interesting to think that my feelings about fresh grass, can be
something else to someone else

Hey

Hey, my brother
You nearly walked into that lamppost
That cyclist almost knocked you down
The 74 bus came close to running you over
A pickpocket's hand just reached for your pocket

Hey you
Can't you see me "I'm streaking, my boobs are out!
You've just walked past that wad £20 notes on the ground
Can't you smell that dog poo! you've just stepped in!!

Hey my sister
You just missed that massive pothole in the pavement.
Didn't you see that beggar asking you for a tenner!
You just missed the Pope waving at you!

All because you are on Twitter, Facebook, WhatsApp, Instagram,
Snapchat on your Smartphone
HEY Bloody look up!!

Holding Hands

Couples
Children
Mother and child
Entwined fingers
Touch
Closeness
Father & child
Lovers
Secret Lovers
Safe
Protection
Carers
Teachers on school trips
School children on a outing
Guiding
Blind
Lost
I'm here for you
Mushy
In love
Grandparents
Grandchildren
So sweet
Romantic
Whoa!!
Affection
I'll look after you
I'm scared
I need you

Tick Tock

Woke up today
hearing the ticking of a clock,
drawn to its sound
tick tock, tick tock
Time is passing,
don't waste it

There's a small white clock,
not seen it before.
Clock in every room,
Two in the living room,
Big one in the kitchen,
Two in the bathroom,
One just ticks, you can't tell the time,

Ticking is good to hear,
while you're relaxing in bathroom doing your business!
Hearing clocks ticking,
can be your music,
Forget digital clocks, with their red LED numbers.

Tick Tock draws you in,
Tick Tock hypnotises you,
Tick Tock makes you still,
Tick Tock you are here and now.
You can't tell what the time is
If you don't look,

Tick Tock lets you know
Time is running
Time is passing
Stop wasting Time
Tick Tock
Tick Tock
Tick Tock

Proud To Be Black

Aren't you proud to be black
We are black and proud
Proud of our different shades of blackness
Proud of our black short and long hair
Proud of our flat noses, our uniqueness
We want to be black and proud
Don't want to be anything else
Want to stay black and proud
Proud of wearing bright African prints and colours
Proud of showing our strong shoulders,
Proud of our thick luscious lips,
Proud of wearing beautiful earrings and necklaces
Proud of our large buttocks
Proud of our creativity as a people
Proud of our black heritage
Proud of our love as a race and people
I'm proud to be black very proud.
Yes I'm Black and Proud

I've Landed

I've walked
I've stared
I've strolled
I've breathed.
I've landed

I've sniffed the sweet fruit, just picked
I've blinked in the bright shining sun
I've sat in the Atlantic Ocean, it's waves trying to draw me in.
I've landed

I've drank the juice of the natural coconut
I've listened to the rustling leaves
I've sucked the sugar cane.
I've landed

I've heard the night sounds of insects
I've frightened away the black & orange lizards, who were staring at me!
I've rubbed the African soil all over my hands
I've landed

I've breathed the mountain air as I've travelled up from Acura Flats to the Hills.
I've smelt the fish just caught
I've woken to the cock crowing, what a wonderful alarm clock. I've landed

I've seen the smile of babies strapped around their mother's backs
I've eaten the pineapples from the street traders, so sweet, so sweet.
I've talked, well tried too, to my African brothers and sisters
I've landed!

I've caress the soft sand from Labadi beach on my feet
I've tasted the mangoes off the trees
I've felt the wind on my skin, cooling me down
I've landed

I've smelt the stench of Tema Bus Station
I've stood at the "Door of No Return" sensing my ancestors' pain.
I've felt the sting of mosquito bite
I've landed

I've ran through the African rain, feeling its warmth
I've watched women balancing their wares on they heads
I've landed

I've smiled at the sun, giving praises, I'm here in Mama Africa
I've landed.

Karibu – Welcome

Karibu to Africa again,
Karibu the breeze is saying, flowing through the leaves,
Karibu your back, we've missed you
Karibu from the ocean waves, rushing in to greet me
Karibu from white sands, green lawns, large foliage,
Karibu from the crickets, chattering she's back
Karibu from the sun as it shines bright, I've missed you.
Karibu my forgotten child, glad to see you again
Karibu from the glowing moon, where have you been
Karibu from the monkeys perched on my veranda wall
Karibu from the stars in the stark black sky twinkling together
Karibu Empress P

Lesson in Parenting No. 1

Screaming on the ground
It's cold, people asking if you are ok, crying, screaming, wailing.
Concerned adults
People looking on
Wonder where the sound was coming from
I can see little girl, with Macdonald's crown
Screaming loud   on her knees
A person shouts out "is this someone's child"?
A couple shouts "back she's ours. She's alright"
Still crying and screaming
Like she is being murdered
Those words, "she's alright"
Sum's up it's a tantrum situation
Discipline or ACD
Leave her be
She wants something
Parents not giving in
Nor is she
Still screaming, still crying
On this bitterly freezing morning
Her knees must be cold
Her face is wet from her tears
Parent looking on
Not caving in
Parenting lesson being taught
It's about watching and learning
Who is the parent?
Who is the child?
 I can see it's breaking the mother's heart
It must be done
It's still chilly
Child still crying and screaming,
Another woman asks if she's ok?
Parent shouts back again,
She's mine.
The woman looks back, her face says "I understand"
Another women looks and says
" you're too hard"
Who said parenting was easy,
It's the importance of discipline or
You'll have hell to pay when she's 11!

The child's crying starts to ease,
She's sniffling now
Wrapping her arms around herself,
Trying to keep herself warm
She realises she's missed out on the hot chocolate
From Macdonald's, her brothers were warm inside.
The cold is biting her now,
Mum and Dad still looking on,
Mum is standing there,
not budging,
I think she is saying to her child,
You have to learn your lesson.
Having a tantrum,
screaming and yelling
You'll lose out.
Mother thinks you are now cold,
You've got a runny nose that needs wiping!
Having a tantrum doesn't work
I'm the parent
You're the child
I have to say no, at times,
You may not like that,
You the child must accept it.
Child, you are now cold,
You are now miserable,
It's not my fault
As your mother I must show discipline.
Another lesson in Parenting.

Mojo

Mojo you've gone, come back
I miss you
I yearn for you
I need you

Mojo where have you gone
Don't you miss me?
Don't you miss pushing me?
Forcing me,
Encouraging me,

Mojo you've gone and taken my passion with you
I am lost without you
I'm sad,
I'm empty,
I'm lonely

Mojo please come back
I need you to elevate me,
I need your conscious vibes
I need your positive words

Mojo come back and
excite me,
stimulate me

I need you back in my veins,
in my nerves,
in my soul,
in my bones,
in my chakras Mojo

Mojo You must miss me, please come back
You know you energize me,
You make me ecstatic
You make me creative

Mojo why did you go?
Why did you run away?

Why did you disappear?
Why did you leave me?

Mojo I need your passion,
I need your zeal
I need your intensity,

Mojo come back
I'm nothing without you,
I'm a lost soul
I'm empty inside

Mojo come back,
Mojo I need you.

My Son

On the day you were born
I can't believe I created you,
You are from me
Loud and screaming like me
Time has flown by
Many first times!!
Feeding yourself
Walking
Running
Dressing
Brushing your teeth,
First day at school

Football games
Basketball games,
Cricket matches
How time has flown
I look at pictures
All those memories
So wonderful so sweet
I created you
I am so proud of you
You have made me what I am today
You are powerful, confident, triumphant, creative, positive, because I am
your mum.
Time has flown, we've been through a lot
But you make me so proud to be your mum.
You've boosted me when I've been down
Been with me through the 'C'.
Helped me when I've had a diabetic episode, getting me off the floor,
back into bed.
Listened to my woes about men, work, women, clothes exercise, love,
life!
Explained how it is never too late to learn.
Given me that hug when I needed it.

My son, I love you, I am so blessed to be your mother.

Sun's Out !

It's time we had sunshine in Brum,
It's time for some warmth,
It's time to smile,
It's time for some vitamin D,

It's time to get home to do the barbecue, yes it's that time!

It's time, get to the garden centre, buy all you need, seeds, plants, even a new mower!

It's that time, put the washing out on the line, watch the breeze blowing out the wetness.

It's time to cut the lawn, smell the grass's freshness, see how quick the cutgrass draws out!!

It's time to weed and turn the soil, watch the birds ready to snatch the worm!

It's time to disturb the frog, that's been resting in the long grass, see it jump away, all green and slimy.

It's time to see ladies in bright pinks, yellows and blues, showing off their arms and legs.

Its time to go to the park, round up the kids, grab a ball, let's play on the grass, on the swings, on the merry go round, It's that time

It's time to listen out for the ice cream van, with its jolly tune 'ice cream man is here'

It's time to buy a 99 ice cream cone, with a flake and raspberry juice.

It's time to gobble and lick it down before it melts, but I want to take my time!

It's time to eat some juicy mangoes, feeling the juices running down your fingers and arms, making them sticky

It's time to enjoy the sunshine,
Weather forecast says,
Going to be thunder and rain tomorrow.

Not Another News Story!

Turn on BBC or Sky News, Al-Jazeera, CNN, Fox News Channels and what do I hear!

Another bomb explodes
Another boat capsizes with migrants
Another woman hasn't come home
Another story about abuse in our children's homes
Another story, young people will have to stay at home past age of 30
Another Story you'll need save thousands of pounds for a house deposit
Another story, hospitals can't cope, not enough nurses, not enough doctors, not enough beds
Another story, stop eating or drinking that because it causes cancer
Another story our food is poisonous and can kill you
Another story, more people are using Food Banks
Another story of a crooked politician abuses his/her power, taking kick backs
Another story, a plane crashes, and it can't be found
Another story people being killed because there are not the right religion
Another story, police shooting another innocent black person in the US
Another story of famine in Africa, thousands are dying, for lack of drinking water
Another Story oil is cheap but gas prices are still high and rising
Another story, a suicide bomber, blows up another airport departure lounge
Another story, more people are sleeping rough, because there are homeless

All these news stories, none of happiness, none about peace, none about love

I refuse to turn on a news channel, because I don't want to hear another bloody sad news story

Pigeon

Pigeon you're brave
You keep walking into this warm coffee shop,
Stepping in so bold
Just looking for a little bit of food,
Baristas shooing you out,
Three days on the trot,
you've come into this Starbucks
So fearless!
You're sensible.
You know it's warm,
You see the bright light,
Is that a sign!
You keep on strolling in!
They keep on shooing you out!
Pigeon you're brave,
Is it the coffee smell?
Yes it's so tempting

That's Starbucks marketing for you!

You've Got How Many!!!

I'm snowed under with all these shoes
Black ones
Flat ones
Wedges
Trainers - Adidas, Nike, Reebok
Flip-flops – Havannas, Gap
Lace ups
Indian sandals
Stilettos
Ankle straps
High thigh boots
Ankle boots,
Black patent boots
Plastic sandals
Doc Martin boots
Doc Martin sandals
Chunky wedge sandals and shoes
Birkenstocks sandals
Gladiator sandals
Too many to choose from
Too many, I'm running out of space
Too many colours, red, blue, green, silver, gold, black, copper, brown
pink, multi coloured!!
You can only wear one at a time
One pair of shoes in different colours,
Too many, too many
How many you said! 175
How many, repeat that again! 175
How many, you must be joking!
Is your middle name 'Imelda Marcos'
How many, where do you put them - under the bed, in the wardrobe both
of them, in a row against the wall, in shoe boxes, in a very large shopping
bag!!
How many 175
How many did you say!
How many 175
How many times do you wear them?
How many colours!!!
How many styles in different colours??
How many!!!!!
175

Shout, Scream and Release

Releasing the tension
Shout
Scream
Getting Out of Babylon
Shout, Scream and Release

Pain
Rage
Anger
Frustration
Shout, Scream and Release

Demoralisation
Tension
Negativity
Snapping
Shout, Scream and Release

Devil
Demons
Short Fuse
Frustration
Shout, Scream and Release

Irritation
Madness
The System
Shout, Scream and Release

Clear your head
Relax
Slow breathing
Relax
Muscles loosen
Calmer
No more shouting and screaming
Just Release

Sound Girl

You fascinate me Mr Selector
Knowing when to drop the needle on that 45
Just when to drop that Johnny Clarke track,
You know how to read us datwas and brothers in the dance
I can't stop staring at you Mr Selector,
The way you flick through your record box, Mr Selector,
I want you to play a Dubplate by Dennis Brown, done specially for your
sound 'SuperPower'
No I am not going to move
I want to watch the controller, mix up the bass and treble
Sensing the vibes from the crowd
The lights on the equipment flashing 'SuperPower'
Look at the amp!
Whole those knobs, those lights

Can't stop staring
Smelling the sensi around me,
Just right as you play Culture's 'Two Seven Clash'

You've done it Mr Selector and Mr Controller
I'm now a Sound Girl

Marching On

I'm marching in life's army
Stepping to salvation
Stepping up for life

I'm getting on the path
I can see my reward
With each step I'm taking
I'm getting there

I'm marching
I'm stepping
I'm striding

Marching like a warrior
I'm stepping like a fighter
Moving to my goal
Progressing to my destiny

We are all getting there
Stepping with my sisters
Marching with my brothers
Walking with our elders
Being blessed by our ancestors
Stepping together

Yes, we are winning this battle
Marching for life

Stop Telling Me

Voices telling me what to do and think
Voices that won't leave me alone, questioning me what are you doing
Voices screaming in my head
Voices wanting me to walk a different way
Voices, chatting, chatting, chatting
Voices telling me What To Do
Voices making me call myself crazy
Voices just keep on saying negative words to me
Voices telling me that I am not worthy
Voices saying that I am not loved
Voices telling me that I'm ugly
Voices telling me I'm fat
Voices telling me I'm too Thin
Voices telling my skin is too dark, I must be fair, must bleach my skin to be accepted
Voices telling me I haven't good hair!!
Voices shouting at me, I must have long blond European hair
Voices screaming at me I must hate myself
Voices telling me I must cut and make myself bleed.
Voices Stop!
I don't want to hear your hateful voices anymore
I want to hear positive uplifting voices saying
I am gorgeous
I am powerful
I am lovely
I am wonderful
I am kind
I am confident
I am beautiful
I am fine just the way I AM.

Talking To My ******

Tell me something, why when you are talking to me you are looking at my breast
Tell me something why can't you talk to my face
Tell me something has my breast got two eyes, one nose, one mouth
Tell me something, has my breasts got a mouth that is talking or answering you back?
Tell me something, what would happen if I was talking to your penis? What would you think?
Tell me something, no eye to eye contact
Tell me something, is my breasts telling you what my day has been like or what my favourite food is or what kind of music I like?
Tell me something, why do you talk to my breast?
Are my breast answering you back?
Tell me something, don't you want to have a conversation with my mouth, eyes, nose, actually with me?
Tell me something, can't you look up and talk to me not my breast

No you can't, you are only 4 foot 6 inches tall!!!

The C

This poem is called 'The C', dedicated to those that have experienced cancer personally through family and friends.

I don't accept it
You've invaded me
I don't want you anywhere in me
You're not welcome
But you don't want to leave
You want to stay, so you tell me
It's my turn, to be the 1 in 3 people to get it. 'The C'

You only stayed for a while,
We battled, through various stuff,
Had couple of operations
Three months of chemo injections
Loss of body hair, had no eyebrows, eyelashes or nasal hair!
You made my nails turn black then they fell out
You made my ackee and saltfish taste like metal
Had to have seventeen days of two minutes of blasts of radiation

We battled through; I wasn't going to let you win this
You made me stronger, but I want you to leave now

Don't come back, you are not welcome!!

Yes, you have made me a survivor,
You've made me a fighter
I'm not scared of you
You've made me face my challenges

Is that why you came? To toughen me up.
Not to take life for granted,

It worked! I can face anything!

As of today I'm one of the 97% survivors of 'Breast Cancer'

Jerry This Is War!!

You really think you can mess with me?
You really think I can't see you?
You really think you can come in here and tek weh yu noh work fa?
You really think I don't know when you've been here? me can see when my things gane down?
You think you are smart? sneaking in when you tink me out
You really think me noh know when yu been here? dropping your bits and bobs
You think you're smart, but this is War

Me have a line of attack in place fe yu
Me have an ambush set for when yu try and pick mi stuff again
You really think yu clever?
You really think yu can invade me space?
You really believe me noh noh know seh yu tell your friends and family about me territory; I bet you use facebook or twitter
You really think, me can't hear yu a search up me room for tings, a crackle here a rustle there.
You really think me can't smell you,
You really think me can't tell when yu send in your spy dem, to see if de coast is clear
Me set fe yu, this is WAR Tom will get you!

You really think that me will give up after the first battle, yu crazy!
You really think yu can send in more of ya pardie dem, to infiltrate me yard,
I set fe yu and your posse this is WAR, Tom will Get You!

You really think yu nippy and swift, but me gwan Catch you click! Click! Click! Click! Tom will get you!

Touch

I'm waiting to kiss those soft succulent lips

Waiting to rub my fingers in your hairy chest, the thought makes me tingle

I can't wait to run my tongue down your lean neck, along your shoulders, I can feel you shudder

My hands waiting to massage your back, starting just there, on your shoulder blade,

I'll be gentle, don't want to startle you

I'm just waiting to run my forefinger up and down your spine I want to sense your quiver

I can't wait to let my thumb stroke you just there between your hip and leg, you're looking sacred

I'm waiting to massage your love handles, that's going to be nice

Yes, I'm waiting to rub my nose over your taut stomach, smelling your 'just bathed' scent

Yes, I'm waiting to stroke my feet along your smooth thighs, don't be afraid

I want to knead your firm buttocks with my smooth hands, I can't wait

I'm waiting to kiss
I'll surprise you!

We Are Sistas

As a woman it is important to have female friends, sistas/ sisters/ mates/ BFF/ girlfriends around you in all aspects of your everyday life. This word of expression tell you all what we are missing when we don't have a sisters around us

Sisters we need you to keep us strong and powerful, with your love and kindness

My Sisters where would I be without your friendships and support

Your Sisters that we can go clubbing, and partying, with, when we need to let your hair down

Sisters are not just our mates, BFF, sisterns, there are our mothers, grandmas, aunties and godmothers

Sisters that we chat or moan to about the husband, boyfriend, man, partner

Our Sisters are great

Your sisters that are your crew, there in the front row, when you are giving that inspiring performance

Your sisters that give you that big round of applause when you've delivered that almighty speech.

My Sisters, there for you when you are feeling absolutely pissed off with life, at your front door with the bottle of wine or Haagen Daz ice cream

Sisters that are challenging the male dominance of our world-wide democracies

Our Sistas telling you when you are wrong , being honest and upfront.

Sisters that tell you YES, your butt does look big in that orange dress!!

Your Sisters that tell you No those shoes don't fit, stop squeezing your feet into them!
My sisters you can rant to about the maddening thing your kids have done again

Our sisters, you can confide in, about your horrible boss Mr Brown, having his hands on your shoulder just a bit too long for the hundredth time.

Your sisters motivating you to rise up, no matter what.

Sisters we can talk to about ever changing dilemmas with our bodies, 'am I putting on too much weight' "why does my breast sag like cow udders" " is it best to pluck or shave the hairs that are growing on my chin!

Your Sisters you need to talk to when you've been told you've got cancer, telling you that you are a survivor and they are there with you all the way.

My Sistas that share each other's womanly health problems, like the arthritis; the high blood pressure; the diabetes; the fibroids.

Your Sistas holding each others' hands and crying as we say farewell to another sistren that has lost her fight with life.

Our sisters around the world that are achieving so much against hostile barriers and opposition

Sisters that are empowering each other, for the right to be treated as an equal.

Our sisters who offer their shoulders for you to lean or cry on, when another one of our children is lost to the knife or gun.

My Sistas, that tell you it's ok to take 5 steps back to take 10 steps forward to reach your dreams

Sistas that see you without the make up, without the extensions, without the wig, without the spandex

Your Sistas that go with you to A & E, when he's punched you again, breaking another bone

My Sisters that just give you a hug without you asking for one, sensing that it is just what you needed.

We are all sisters, regardless of race, regardless of age, regardless of faith

We are all connected, around the world, through the universal energy of life

We are sisters

What A Smell!

What a smell!
What a stench!!

Pong of sleeping rough lord oh god!
What a smell on the bus
It's stinging my eyes ,

You are unable to wash to get rid of the dirt and whiff
What a smell!

One sock's
What a frossy smell

One shirt
What a sweaty smell

Why did he have to sit down beside me!

One underpants
What a stinking smell

One sleeping bag
What a rancid smell

One pair of shoes dem stink

What a smell
I wonder if he knows him smell
Surely him know

Should I be angry and tell him to find another seat
Or
Should I be sympathetic, give him some money
Which one should I choose?

Is It Love?

Is it feeling lost,
Is it being needy
Is it wanting that touch
Is it hearing a voice, so intoxicating
Is it a giggle or laugh, sets you off feeling queasy
Is it that touch, rough or smooth
Is it that smell, a perfume, or after-shave,
Is it that walk, confident and proud,
Is it touching the hair, so soft, so regal, feeling your Samson strength
Is it rubbing the baldness of your head, so smooth!
Is it the feel of fingers touching or stroking
Is it your stomach feeling that flutter of butterflies
Is it the sound of someone calling your name, sensual and exciting!
Is it reflecting on the sweet memories or flashbacks, whoa!
Is it Love, I hope so!

Beauty

Who sees your beauty?
When you are covered from head to toe
All I can see is your eyes

I can't see the shape of your nose or lips,
Can't see if you've got short or long hair, is it glossy!
Whose sees your beauty? When you are covered from head to toe!
Only can see your eyes
Can't see your hands or your feet

Why do you wear black? I know its slimming!
Even when the sun is shinning
Aren't you hot when you're covered from head to toe!

Is it your religion?
Is it your husband?
Is it your father,
Is it your brother?
Is it your mother?
Is it your holy book that says you must be covered

You are a woman, created by your creator
Why can't I see your loveliness?
You know beauty is in eye of beholder
Your beauty should be seen by all,
are you ashamed of your radiance?

Why are you covered all over?
I can't only see your beauty

Do I need to see your beauty
I can feel your beauty as it oozes in the air

Reggae Women

Reggae music by women, telling us about love, peace, family, identity, sisterhood, harmony survival, Africa
Reggae sistrens your voices are so attractive, hearing your sweet tones.
Reggae women – you lift me up with the spirit of your powerful words
Reggae women – your singing is about you and me
Reggae dawtas your music soothes me
Reggae women you are my history telling me about your struggles and triumphs – hear Joy White in her song **Tribulation 'Girls must go through tribulation no matter who or where she's from'**
Reggae princesses – you are the rhythm of my life
Reggae women your passion runs through my veins
Reggae women –you inspire me like when **Judy Mowatt sings Slave Queen ' move the shackles from your mind'**
Reggae queens using your voices to express your emotions
Reggae women – telling me to love myself, always
Reggae empresses uplifting me with your lyrics
Reggae women you are empowering me with your exquisite words,
Reggae women you are my blackness just listen to **Kofi's Black Pride - 'Black is the colour of my skin, Black is the life I live'**
Reggae princesses telling me I am beautiful,
Reggae empresses – conveying to me that I am powerful, **Listen to Queen Ifrica 'Lioness on the rise don't ever have doubt'** motivating me to rise
Reggae women encouraging me to be better person in the eyes of my creator
Reggae sistas thank you for bringing me your words, sound and power.
Reggae women singing to me about powerful love of my Kingman. **Hear Jean Adebambo's lyrics 'You make my life such a Paradise'**
Reggae dawtas, singing to me about the excitement of being in love hear **JC Lodge 'Someone Loves You Honey '**
Reggae women – expressing your senses in your lyrics, so powerful
Reggae women telling us about the same romantic experiences I'm going through just like when **Louisa's sings 'two cousins don't kiss especially like this' Caught You In A Lie**
Reggae queens – singing about my love of a man, even when he stops loving me **hear Marcia Griffiths sings 'Sweet Bitter Love, What have you awaken in me'**
Reggae women Look at me now, look how far I've come, showing that I can survive no matter what
Reggae sistrens passing the baton to our Daughters, Nieces, God Daughters and Granddaughters,

Reggae women you inspire me to keep on achieving my dreams and goals. Listen **Judy Mowatt when she sings 'Feel The Spirit, Lord I thank you'.**

Reggae women your lyrics always reminding me of my spiritual worth Reggae princesses telling me that I am royal & majestic,

Reggae women – reminding me not to be afraid I will survive hear **Etana tells us ' No I, I'm Not Afraid No 'if dem come let dem come because I am protected by the most I one'**

Reggae women you give me joy and hope with your songs

Reggae women singing to me about our motherland Africa hear Christine sing '**Mama Africa, I'm coming home where the milk and sweet honey flow'**

Reggae dawtas your songs setting me free from the Babylon system hear it when **Marcia sings 'Stepping Out Of Babylon one by one, Stepping in Mount Zion'**

Reggae sistrens your melodies making me want to dance like when Marcia screams out '**Feel Like Jumping'**

Reggae women – when you toast/dj your lyrics there's a positive rhythm, so cool, **Listen to Patra's 'Queen of the Pack' and Tanya Stephens 'You Nuh Ready for Dis Yet'**

Reggae women singing about a mother's love of her children hear **Etana words 'Youts a hold dem roots' from her iconic track 'Roots'**

Reggae empresses - you challenge the system like when **Marla Brown sings 'Rise up, Rise Up, Rise Up Rise Up , join the unification and show them Better days will come for dem'** ,

Reggae women – You are Me and I am You

I love you Reggae Women

Different Shades of Blackness

Afro,
Thick lips,
Flat Broad Nose
Rhythm,
Dub
Loud,
Emotional,
Ageless,
Coordinating Colours,
Struggle
Vibrant colours,
Pain,
Massive grin,
Dread locks,
Chains
Red, Gold & Green,
Red, Black & Green,
Quick
Ital
Athletic,
African,
Sorrow
Oppressed
Buzzing,
Cool,
Smooth skin,
Stylish
Cocoa Butter,
Ebony,
Black History,
Reggae
Racism
Wrap head
Creative
Musical
Large buttocks,
Soul music
Shackles
Jazz
Nubian
Kenti

Swahili
Powerful
Nation of Islam
Bondage
'kiss teeth',
curry goat,
'cut eye',
Kwanzaa,
Revolution,
Drumming
Bass
Fried Chicken
Patois
Suffering
Baldhead
Black Power,
Black Panthers,
Rastafari
Plaits
Head Scarves,
Greasy faces,
Cocked batty
Strong
Cane Row hair style,
Slavery
Black 'a' Moor
SUS Laws
Suspicious
Proud
Hardworking
Misunderstood Bubbly
Natural
Jah
Beautiful
Love

Waiting For A Dance

That song is playing John Holt "Stick by Me"
Stick by me and I'll stick by you
Marie gets pull for a dance
Janice get dragged off
Sandra goes next!
Carol is the next go
Would you believe it my brother Donald gets asked
I'm on my own,
I'm swaying to 'Stick by me, I'll stick by you'
I want a dance
Imagining a man's arms around me
I'm waiting
A guy walks towards me
Hurry up I said to myself!
But he walks past me! Pulls a girl behind me
The DJ pull up the track again
'Stick by me, I'll stick by you'
Great another chance
I'm dancing on my own
Making out I don't care, big grin on my face!
Singing the lyrics out loud,
But I want a dance with a man
'Stick by me, I'll stick by you'
Still I'm waiting for that touch on my elbow
Or the hand on my waist turning me around
The DJ Pull up the track for the 2nd time
Stick by me I'll stick by you'
Then I get a touch on my elbow,
I turn around, I can't wait to start
But it's my cousin Patrick asking me if I want a drink!!
The look of disappointment on my face!!
I'm vex, I wanna dance with a man to this song
I go over to the dj,
Grab the mike, scream out to every man on his own
I WANT A DANCE!!
I then lift up the needle, put it down at the start
To play Stick by me AGAIN
I walk with my head held high to stand by a wall
Hoping that someone will have pity on me
And then this short brother come towards me and ask 'can I beg you a dance'!!

Of course I say YES, all I want is a Dance!!
Stick by me and I'll stick by you!

Live Good Today

Give Praise
Live in harmony and peace
Love everyone
Love everything
The time is now
Time is running

Give with love
Live good today
Live good always
Have forgiveness
No enemies
No conflict
Live good

Be kind
Be compassionate Live Good
Be virtuous Live good
Be respectful Live Good

People of the world Live Good
Love your fellowman and woman
Wherever you are live good
Live Good Live Good today

Live in kindness
Live in Peace
Live in Harmony
Live in Joy
Live good today, it will follow you
ALWAYS

VERSE FROM APS PUBLICATIONS
(www.andrewsparke.com)

Printed in Poland
by Amazon Fulfillment
Poland Sp. z o.o., Wrocław

54439289R00034